Zoo Day
Claire Henley

Dent Children's Books

London

We're all going to the zoo.

There is the zoo-keeper.
He rubs and scrubs the
elephant's wrinkled grey back.

Then he fetches juicy bamboo shoots
for the big, black and white panda.

The hairy gorilla likes fruit.
Look at him beat his chest!

We throw fish to the sleek seals.
They splash in and out of the water.

Then we wave to
the snow-white polar bears
playing with their cubs.

Now it's time to ride
the sand-coloured camels.
They walk slowly and sleepily
behind their keeper.

There are the spotted cheetahs
prowling to and fro.

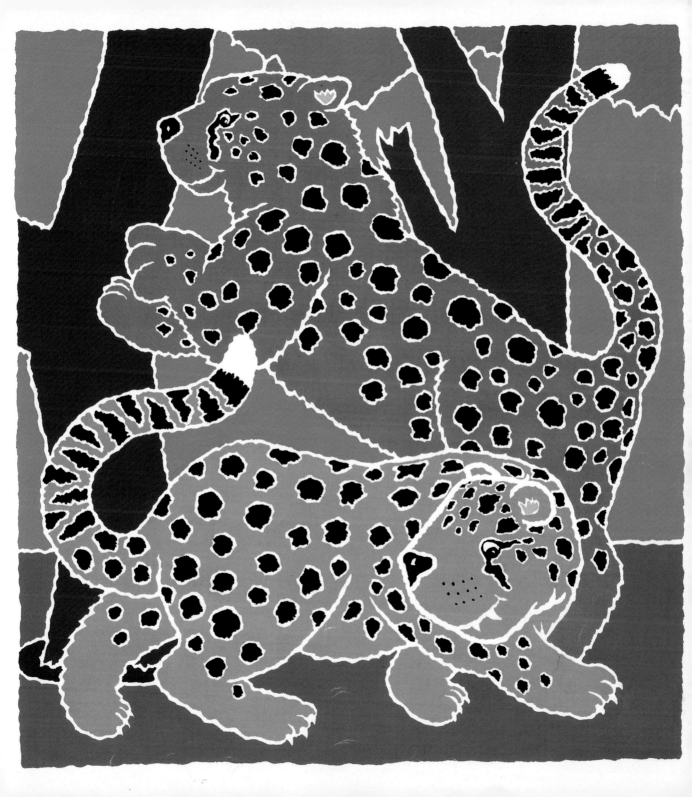

The peacock parades its
fan of feathers.
The humming-birds hover.

The hungry tigers growl and roar.
It's feeding time.

The huge, horned rhinos
have clean straw for their bed.

There's just enough time to
see the chimpanzees,
then wave good-bye to everyone!